W9-AFZ-140

Minibeasts

by Tammy J. Schlepp

Copper Beech Books
Brookfield, Connecticut

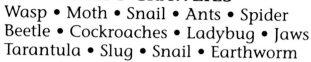

Contents

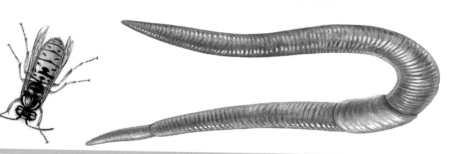

© Aladdin Books Ltd 2000

Designed and produced by
Aladdin Books Ltd
28 Percy Street
London W1P 0LD

First published in
the United States in 2000 by
Copper Beech Books,
an imprint of
The Millbrook Press
2 Old New Milford Road
Brookfield, Connecticut 06804

ISBN 0-7613-1223-4

Cataloging-in-Publication data is on
file at the Library of Congress

Printed in U.A.E.

Coordinator
Jim Pipe

Design
Flick, Book Design and Graphics

Picture Research
Brian Hunter Smart

Come one! Come all!

Welcome to the world of minibeasts!

Do you know what they do?

They crawl, fly, and bite.

Do you know who they are?

Turn the page and say "hi"

to a spider and a fly!

Minibeast

Wasp

Have you ever wondered what it would be like to be tiny?

Lots of these minibeasts are smaller than a penny! Look at this moth on a hand.

Some minibeasts are bigger.

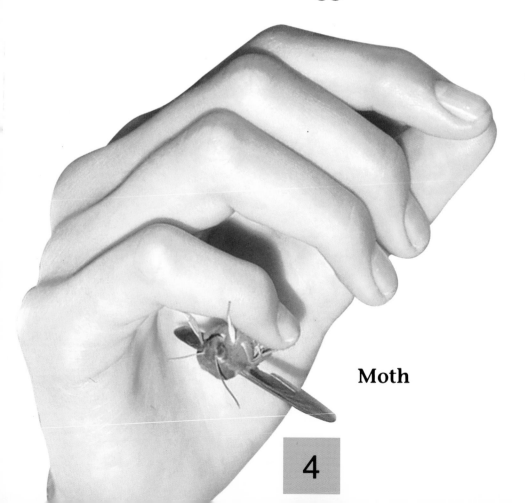

Moth

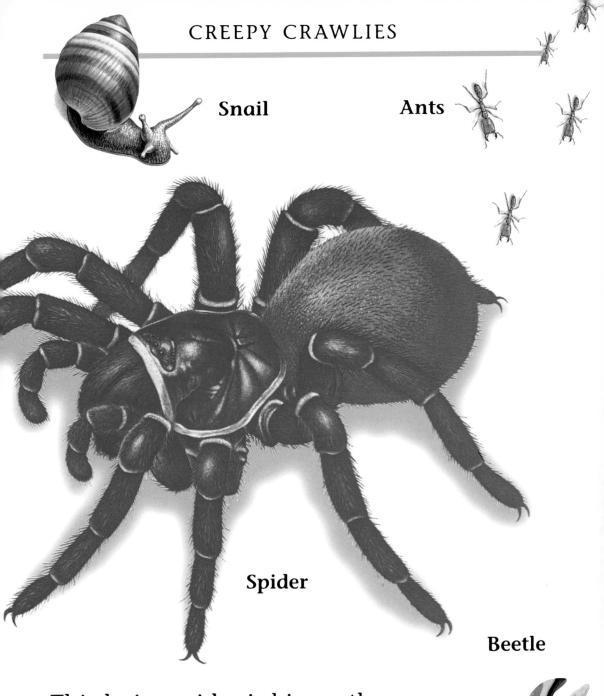

Snail

Ants

Spider

Beetle

This hairy spider is bigger than your hand. Would you like to hold it?

Do you like to run fast?

You could be a cockroach. You could hide
all day and come out at night. Leftover
food would make a good dinner!

A ladybug isn't as fast on its feet—but it
can fly through the sky.

Cockroaches

Ladybug

Where are its wings?

Not every spider is poisonous.
But they all look scary!

Spiders crawl fast on their eight legs.
Watch out!

They have fangs at the end of
their jaws.

Jaws

Tarantula
A spider has
eight legs.

9

Do you like to play in a garden?
You could be a slug or snail and
eat a leaf for lunch.

Slugs and snails don't have legs.
They have a foot that they crawl
on slowly.

Snails carry their home
with them—it's the
shell on their back!

Slug

Snail

Worms don't have legs either.

But they can wiggle fast!

Look at this earthworm's pink body

wiggle in the soft dirt.

Earthworm

Beetles! Beetles! Everywhere! They live in deserts and mountains and places in between.

Beetle

Beetles also have wings for flying. They find their food with their feelers. They are not fussy eaters. They'll even eat rugs!

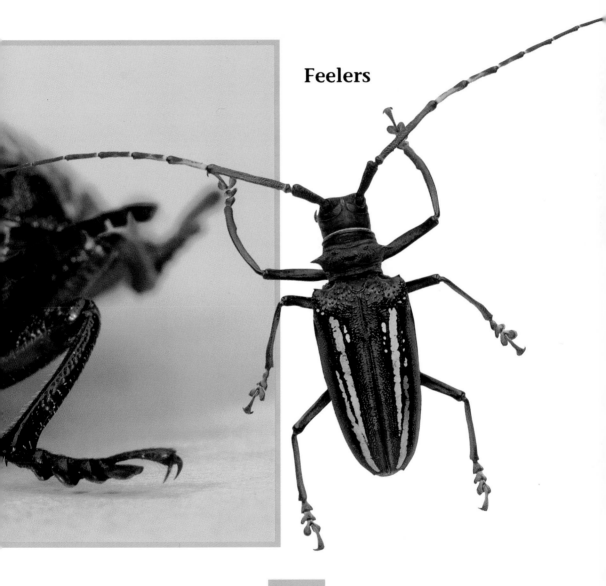

Feelers

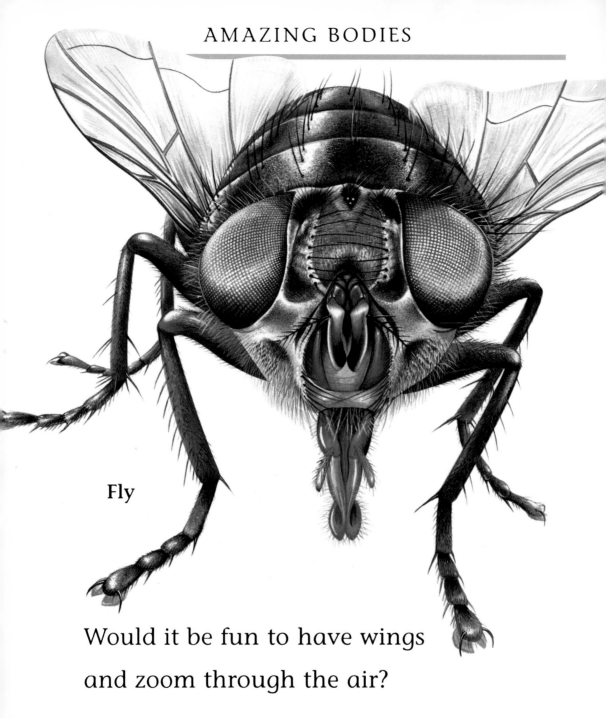

Fly

Would it be fun to have wings
and zoom through the air?

You could be a buzzing fly!
"Catch me if you can!"

Flies also have tiny claws and sticky liquid on their feet. That's why they can crawl upside down.

Maggots may look like worms, but they are really baby flies!

Maggots

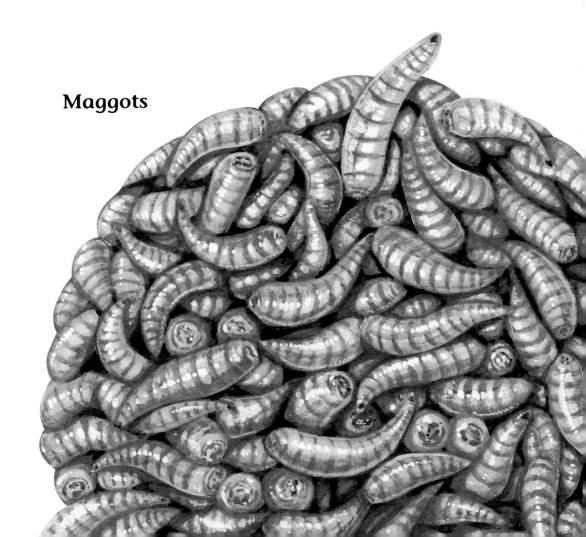

Why do spiders spin silky webs?
To catch their food!

The spider waits for an insect to
get stuck in the web.

Then it wraps the insect up and
eats it later for dinner.

Spinning a web

1   2   3

Moth

Can you see its feelers?

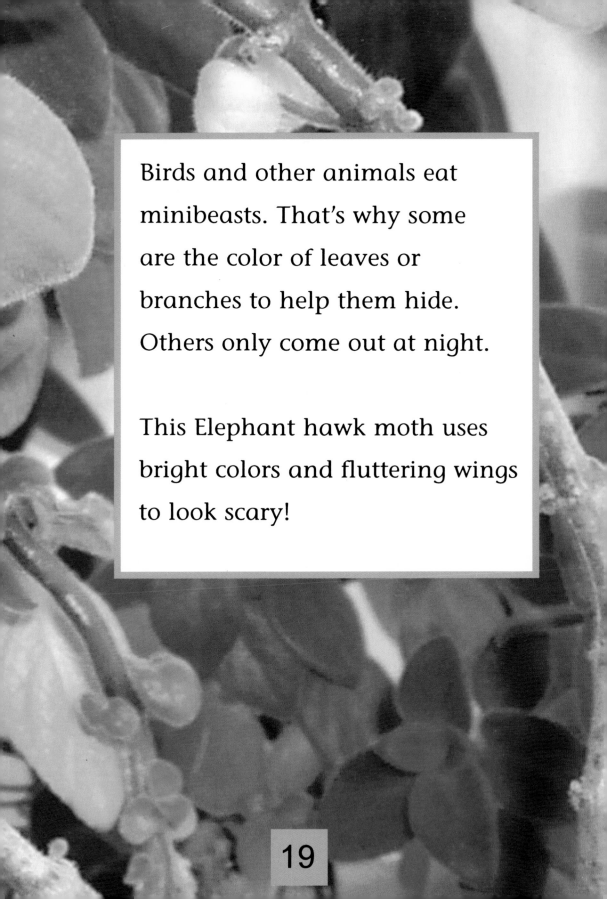

Birds and other animals eat
minibeasts. That's why some
are the color of leaves or
branches to help them hide.
Others only come out at night.

This Elephant hawk moth uses
bright colors and fluttering wings
to look scary!

Stick insect

Now you see me. Now you don't!

Some minibeasts look like plants so that they can hide. Can you find the minibeast in the picture above?

20

"Don't eat me! I taste bad!"

The bright red color on this hairy
caterpillar is a warning to birds.

Caterpillar

"Stay away," says one beetle, "or I'll squirt my poison on you!"

Squirt!

"You stink!" says this hungry mouse as it backs away from the red-and-black stinkbug.

Stinkbugs

Scorpion

Scorpions look like tiny lobsters.
But don't try to eat one.

It uses its tail to sting attackers and to
catch its own dinner.

A scorpion's sting is very painful!

23

Nest

Beware! Wasps are another minibeast with a mean sting.

Wasps work together to build a nest out of leaves, wood, mud, and wax!

Many wasps moving about together are called a swarm.

If you see one, keep away!

Wasps

Everyone has a job in the ant colony.

The queen ant lays eggs.
Worker ants look for food and care for the babies. Soldier ants protect the colony from enemies.

Ants touch one another's feelers to talk.

Ant colony

Can you count them?

Can You Find?

Minibeasts have lots of strange parts that people don't have.

Can you find which minibeast these parts come from?

Wings

Jaws

Shell

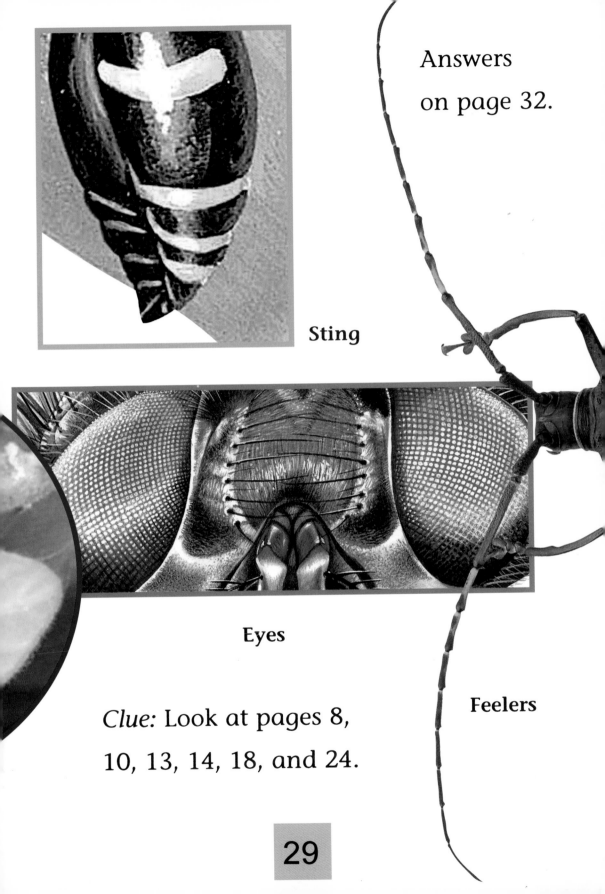

Sting

Answers on page 32.

Eyes

Feelers

Clue: Look at pages 8, 10, 13, 14, 18, and 24.

Do You Know?

Minibeasts can be found in lots of places.

Do you know where these minibeasts live?

The answers are on page 32.

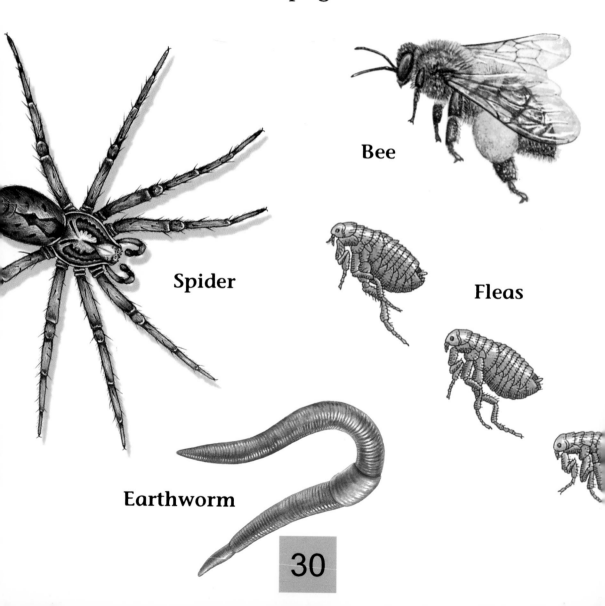

Bee

Spider

Fleas

Earthworm

30

On a web

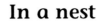
In a nest

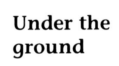
Under the
ground

On a dog

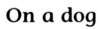

31

Index

ANSWERS TO QUESTIONS

Page 28-29 – A spider has these **jaws** • A snail has this **shell** • A moth has these **wings** • A wasp has this **sting** • A fly has these **eyes** • A beetle has these **feelers**.

Pages 30-31 – A **bee** lives **in a nest** • **Fleas** live **on a dog** • An **earthworm** lives **under the ground** • A **spider** lives **on a web**.

Photocredits: Abbreviations: t-top, m-middle, b-bottom, r-right, l-left.
Cover, 7—Ralph A Clevenger/CORBIS. 1, 3, 8-9, 12—Stockbyte. 4, 6, 11, 18-19, 20, 28r—Select Pictures. 10, 28b—John Foxx Images. 16-17— Corbis. 21—Michael & Patricia Fogden/BBC Natural History Unit. 23—Peter Oxford/BBC Natural History Unit. 25s—Borrell Casals/FLPA-Images of Nature. 26-27—Andrew Cooper/BBC Natural History Unit.
Illustrators: David Cook, Tony Swift, Myke Taylor; Simon Turvey—Wildlife Art Ltd.; Philip Weare, Norman Weaver.